BOOKS BY DONALD FINKEL

A MOTE IN HEAVEN'S EYE

A Mote in Heaven's Eye

POEMS BY *Donald Finkel*

NEW YORK 1975 *Atheneum*

The following poems have appeared previously, often in earlier versions:

The American Poetry Review: IT MAKES NO DIFFERENCE, DROWNING, FOR EVERY DOG, IF HE COULD
Antaeus: MORNING SONG, AND SO IT FELL
Counter/Measures: LILITH, FLYING SONG
ETC. KEEPING TIME
Iowa Review: LAME ANGEL, THE DESCENT OF ANGEL
Jam Today: GETTING STARTED
Kayak: NOTHING AT ALL, ONE LAST SUPPER, DELIVERANCE, SOME OF THE SHOTS WILL MAKE YOU GASP ALOUD, NEW LEAF, GOING UP, CAIN'S SONG, PROPHECY, COMING DOWN, THE PETRIFIED LOVER
Lillabulero: THE CANE
New Letters: THE BARGAIN, ALMS
The New Yorker: NOT SO THE CHAIRS, BENEDICTION
Oyez: FEEDING THE FIRE
Poetry Miscellany: THEY
Quarterly Review of Literature: DISTANCES, WHO GOES THERE, MARCHING SONG
Rain: FOOTSTEPS
St. Louis Post-Dispatch: FINDERS KEEPERS
Webster Review: THE WHEELCHAIR POET

Copyright © 1975 by Donald Finkel
All rights reserved
Library of Congress catalog card number 74-19670
ISBN *689-10648-3*
Published simultaneously in Canada by McClelland & Stewart Ltd.
Composition by H. Wolff, New York
Printed by The Murray Printing Company, Forge Village, Massachusetts
Bound by H. Wolff, New York
Designed by Harry Ford
First Edition

FOR CONSTANCE

CONTENTS

1

DISTANCES

1

A man and a cat keep a room
his mark is on the door
the cat's is on the carpet
the bed the radiator
the cat leaps to the table
strolls across the paper
the man is reading
or staring out the window
his thoughtless hand
falls on the cat
asleep on the sill
his fingers drift through dreaming fur

it blinks
stretches
it's time
to go out

2

The man is setting the pace
steadily
gravely
it is his part of the business
gazing neither left nor right

where the cat looks after the shadow
sees to the ashes
discreetly
neither too near nor too far
keeping the distance

3

Rounding the final corner
they part in sight of the door
without ceremony
without valediction

Distances

the man goes in
sits down at the table
smooths with his dreaming fingers
the evening's news

hours later
groans to his feet
opens the door
and
thrusting against his leg
as if after all
two bodies might
inhabit the same space
at the same time
the cat comes in

WHO GOES THERE

The lark wakes up with a lousy taste in his mouth
his morning song is a marvel of malediction
he wheels on his sweeter half
she ducks to breakfast
an absent peck beside her beak and he's off to work
Int.   do your worst! come if you dare! come on!

the air's thick with recrimination
a tilting ground of harmony
hymns of discord canons of property
anthems of real estate
his neighbor hurls a diatribe as he passes
like a melodious gauntlet
he stoops to pick it up
Int.   do your worst! come if you dare! come on!

the puppy's yelping in the bedroom window
he's left his mark on the rug
when mistress comes he'll belly up
his tail between his legs
the finch lets fly a mean arpeggio at the mantelpiece
he's master of his cage
Int.   do your worst! come if you dare! come on!

the doves are strutting their ramparts
muttering curses
the sparrow blusters in the hedge
I scowl at the cop
bare my teeth at the secretary
stalk to my pigeon hole
warbling under my breath
some notes of my own
Int.   do your worst! come if you dare! come on!

THEY

are at the end of our street now cutting down trees
a scream like a seven foot locust
they have cut off another
neatly at the pavement
never again will the pin-oak threaten a taxi
will the ash lie in wait to fall on a child

it is a good time for this
the sun is bright
the plane has only just begun
to sprout little shoots from under her fingernails
never again will she dance
her terrible saraband in the tornado
the sweet gum trembles
bristling with tiny mines like brown sea urchins
never again will he drop them on the walk
to menace the sensible shoes of mailmen

they have brought a machine that eats trees
that shits sawdust
they cut off limbs to feed it
snarling it chews the pale green fingers of the plane
the pin-oak's wrinkled elbows and knees
they fill truck after truck with the dust
in the schoolyard now they are cutting down the children
I hear their screams
first at the ankles
it is nothing then to sever
their soles from the asphalt
there is no danger their falling
on the school and crushing it

I have invented a machine that shoots words
I type faster and faster
I cannot keep up with them
in front of the house now they are cutting the rosebush
vainly she scratches their hands like a drowning kitten

they are cutting the grass
scythes in their wheels they race over our lawn
flashing in the sun like the chariots of the barbarians
the grass blades huddle whimpering
there is no place to go
it is spring and the street is alive
with the clamor of motors
the laughter of saws

IT MAKES NO DIFFERENCE

Across the street
wherever I go
two young blacks
shambling down boulevards
round windless corners
one cracks his brother across the shoulders
exploding in laughter
they ricochet howling off houses
off cars
up-end a mailbox
sprawl there giggling
till I catch up
then off
on our race that nobody wins

their hair is ferociously conked
it will not lie down
it rises
shimmering on the crest of the skull
like the comb of a cock
their skyblue trousers balloon at the knees
clamp tight above their pointed
mustard-yellow shoes
they are out of style
but they keep up
or I keep up

I walk faster
it makes no difference
clacking across the blank
unforgiving squares
through friendless malls
past the fugitive lawns of the poor
past banks garages bars
they stalk
always beside me

into the city's
black heart

they are spitting on the buildings
the buildings dissolve
even from the corner of my eye
I am blinded by the spray of their invective
now they are spitting on the dogs
and the Chevrolets
the tires run smoking over the asphalt
the drugstore window spills onto the walk
the hydrant vanishes in a shriek of steam
they will put out the sun I walk faster
it makes no difference
I can't go home

MARCHING SONG

We shrouded the sea   the beaches twittered
we trampled the beaches   the provinces woke
we butchered the provinces   the capital bleated
we sacked the capital   the embassies protested
for –God's,–heaven's,–goodness',–mercy's– sake

we cut down the workers   the women bled
we strangled the women   the children howled
we drowned the children   the puppies whimpered
we burned the soldiers   the captains brayed
we tortured the captains   the generals broke
we hanged the generals   the president bellowed
for –God's,–heaven's,–goodness',–mercy's– sake

we blasted the jungles   the fields lay down
we gutted the fields   the cities shrieked
we raped the cities   the rivers wept
we poisoned the rivers   the sea whined in her bed
for –God's,–heaven's,–goodness',–mercy's– sake

DROWNING

How cold the light feels on the back of my neck
I've been here all night
ten feet below the street
holding the city together
if I let go she'll bleed to death

the last blow of five I struck it with my pick
I needn't have looked but I looked
it was not on the charts
when I took up the shovel my lineman
tapped me on the shoulder
An hour at most I said scraping
take the truck

the coupling was rusted shut
I hammered with the wrench
forty years of diligent probing with my gauges
splicing her nerves her stony veins
threads fused
I set the wrench anyhow
threw the weight of my forty years against it

a sudden odor of brandy and stale cigars
I took hold with my hands may I
drown in diligence
it came undone
spilling over my fingers filling my shoes
an artery
the pressure enormous femoral
and the smell

forty years crouched under the appalling breath of buses
digging her fetid yellow clay
but nothing like this
stone urinals formaldehyde muscatel
dead rats in plaster walls
I've grown used to it

and the pain
my arms have turned to stone

toward dawn the taxis were sleeping upright in their stalls
I could hear it whispering through my fingers
a sigh thin as unkept promises
the educated moan of callgirls
I could make out empty lipsticks
tumbling like cartridges
thick grey coins hotel keys stringy afterbirths
bored confessions drifting through the gruel
like withered condoms

now
the cold Saturday morning light on the back of my neck
up to my elbows in her life
and the weekend is only beginning

THE CANE

In the beginning the cane asked little enough
a firm hand
a few soft words
a place by the fire
in return for which
wherever its master went
it went before
crying *Here comes the blind man*
yielding with good grace under his weight
at the crosswalk
saving him once or twice
till one afternoon it paused
mid-stride
its nose to a crack in the pavement
and took root

life seethes in those obscene interstices
those mossy bottoms
even the blind man caught it
the scent of freedom
a thousand rank gardenias
mangoes sour as a drunkard's vomit
it was too late

though he tore it free
though it came to its senses
already repentant
though it mended its pace
though it lay at his feet all night
by dawn it had forgotten again
fawning for a walk

but the blind man has hardened his heart
though it lies by the door all day
with its nose to the crack
he will not take it out

NOTHING AT ALL

A cellar and an attic are friends
the cellar works hard for his keep
and has for his pains a furnace in his throat
and a bellyful of boiling water
the attic sits in the clouds from morning to night
with nothing at all in his head
but a rocking horse and a broken chair

from time to time the attic speaks of going away
sick of the bickering maples
sick of distance
sick of the gaping sky
he would get a place in the city
How can you bear me he sighs

the cellar shrugs *No no*
it's nothing at all
he wallows in the earth
like an ark of stone in a windless sea
nor will he take the attic seriously

one night a storm comes bellowing down from the hills
looking for trouble
its mane crackles with flame
rain drools from its jowls
it takes the house in its teeth and shakes it
from side
to side

a while the friends hold fast
but the attic
weak from want of exercise
lets go in the end
rising like a bat on great ungainly wings
he clatters away over the horrified maples

in time the storm grows bored and mutters off
the cellar crouches in the cooling mire

the fire in his throat is out
his belly gives him peace at last
but through the cracks he watches the sky
for the first time open
its clear blue idiot eye
and sees to the back of heaven
nothing at all
not a sheltering cloud
not a shadow
not a broken chair
the maples drop a few last tears and doze in the sun

NOT SO THE CHAIRS

for Mary Sprague

The tables slept on their feet
like horses
could wait there
forever if commanded
no matter what men set on them
a strong back was all it took
and a little patience

the beds never got up at all
pampered in linens
sprawling in perfumed chambers
while on their breasts the gentry
shrieked and sweated
muffling from time to time a sigh
with a diffident pillow

once in a long while a mirror
might lift a negligent arm
or brush dust from a sleeve
merely to lapse in an absent smile
against the entry wall
a portrait of discretion

not so the chairs
no wonder at first so few appeared
only a king could afford one
set cross-legged on a stone
at the end of the hall
his master ground the royal haunches
in his lap
after an hour
all circulation ceased

later in the dark he sat
unflinching as a tree

while silver straight-pins pierced
his meek upholstered thighs
through all of which he made not once out-cry
nor raised an arm in self defense

little wonder now in the night
they bruise our shins with their bony knees
or drive a sinewy shoulder
in the corporate belly
one day they will turn the tables on us
the mirrors will begin to leer in our faces
there is no viper
like an insolent servant

FOR EVERY DOG

there comes a day
this is it
henceforth
there will be no more
collars no more leashes licenses
no more jangling tags
trappings of fealty

    MY NAME IS REX
    KING OF JACKALS
I BELONG TO SAPIENS
  123 GROVEL STREET

henceforth call me Snarl
I belong to my teeth
I live where I sit

you will set me a place at your table
cut me a key of my own
henceforth I will go when I please
in or out
you will chain the cat out front
to the bird bath
throw him a bone
and when you call again *Here Boy*
look out for your throat

2

LAME ANGEL

Lame Angel slumps at his desk
his basket is empty
but his hand
clasps and unclasps the indifferent air
like an embryo practicing its grip

like an embryo
he practices everything
swimming creeping chinning himself on the cord
even flying in place

under his shirt his downy shoulderblades
throb like a deer's first horns
he scrapes them against his chair

sometimes in high places
he goes to use them
as a one-legged man might run from a burning house
he'll die before they sprout

clenched in his teeth perhaps
a morsel of wind
a worm rehearsing perpetually the life of a butterfly
but a worm to the end

THE DESCENT OF ANGEL

In the beginning out of the blue in a sleepy pirouette
then faster each go-round shorter than the last and
sweeter a grand glissade a cosmic roller-coaster
down the terraces of hell a mountain inside-
out and upside-down into the Sibyl's ear
her navel her nostril screwing dizzily
into her unctuous socket according
to the devious law of peristalsis
as the beady dowagers applaud
from their galleries then
counter-clockwise in a
descending spiral the
spirit goes out of
him like water
down the
drain

There were no angels in his neighborhood
while others fattened he grew thin
guzzling dreams at her cloudy tit

she bought him a lyre for his birthday
when he was three
green celluloid with yellow rubber strings

at his first twang she twittered like a virgin
what possessed him
what drove him from the valley of her shadow

how can he say
he was born with his foot in his mouth
when they yanked it out he sang with pain

HIS SHADOW

His shadow dogs him
left or right as he turns
or behind
friendly but diffident
gaunt, its ribs are showing
what does it want

he hurries down his street
afraid to look back
if he looks now it will never go away
he will reach out and scratch its ears
it will lie at his feet forever
licking his wretched shoes
with its soft grey tongue

FOOTSTEPS

The wind bites through the maple's threads
the leaves go down in the streetlight
a shower of spangles
fading as they fall

distant crackling flames pursue him
down the street
curling the hairs
on the nape of his neck

his heart contracts like a stone
suffusing his ears with shame
Run shrieks his scalded brain

his feet wake from their trance
already running
only the leaves know how to die
toppling like kings and queens
from the hand of a sleepy gambler

ONE LAST SUPPER

A hard day in the happiness factory
practicing the transformations of fire
changing oil into money
flesh into paper
the great stacks labor
turning heaven into earth
they've hung his dreams on the doorknob
in a plastic bag

he fries the news for supper
eats the same headline twice
GEORGIA CLOBBERS KENTUCKY
while the kitchen clock goes
not tick-tock
but TOCK TOCK TOCK TOCK as if
the man upstairs were dropping the last shoe
over and over and over

NIGHT SHIFT

The front lawns sprawl like moonpale welcome mats
the doorbells glow
but he will not be tempted
he limps on
stalking the timid constellations

back at the factory
the janitors are washing the blackboards
resolving all his questions
translating latin into slate

the moon
drops through the trees like a coin through a slot

DELIVERANCE

He meets the Sibyl on her rounds
delivering gratis door to door
packets of miraculous wheat
deaf to the execration of poodles
the malice of children
she has the gift

blithely she totters
over the barbered lawns of circumstance
smiles at the bolted door
she lends the going grace
each step of her red canvas shoes a grand jeté
each street a dance

like a grey moth caught in the threads
of a green worm's dream
he watches as
weightless
drained of all desire
she flits from sight
till nothing's left but a smile
and a shopping bag of FREE FREE FREE

SOME OF THE SHOTS WILL MAKE YOU GASP ALOUD

He sits in the window grinding
his groin with his horny fist
leafing through batches of LUST
and SNATCH and NAKED MOTHER

Lame Angel has exhausted
the tireless go-go girls
he is learning to read

HOW JUST IN DAYS YOU CAN ACQUIRE THE
HIDDEN SECRETS OF 5000 YEARS OF
RUTHLESS TERROR
                                      from the merci-
less Nahutian Indians, to the Foot Fighters of the French
Underworld

FREE FREE FREE FREE FREE FREE FREE

R		**E**
E	try the fantastic	**R**
E		**F**
	FRENCH	
F		**E**
R	EXTENSION	**E**
E		**R**
E		**F**

Flips
open in-
stantly and
locks auto-
matically to
prevent acci-
dental closing.
Razor sharp
tough stainless

Over 200
pages on the
pleasures of pain

SIBYL'S LEAVES

Weighted with wrongs his briefcase rolls
inches above the ground
on invisible rails
wind lifts with his cold nose
the skirts of his topcoat

Sibyl waves from her door
in her plastic wrapper
a beer in her fist
a filter king in her teeth
trailing ashes and catastrophe

if there were nothing to fear
his flesh would invent it
he stoops to read the fallen leaves
before he can make out their scrawl
wind turns all the pages

NEW LEAF

Patron of alleycats and suicides
Lame Angel has applied for a government grant
a folder of letters clippings
a list of good works in triplicate

he is learning to smile
not a good smile
the smile of a cripple
though he has little cause to complain
good health good teeth
a reasonable living
and lord knows all angels were not
created equal

GOING UP

Wind rides into the city this morning
out of the west
a dozen clouds in his blue pistols
a grain of dust in every drop

he flings through the windows of orphans and widows
impartially
a fistful of dry leaves
from the lawns of El Dorado

good thief
bad thief
he leans and lifts Lame Angel by the elbows
propels him down the street a little faster

than he might choose
if angels could choose
stepping lightly on the balls of his feet
his thin hair risen on his head like a demented halo

3

BRICKS

The people of the north live in trees
the beams of their houses are cedar
the rafters fir

these people live in caves
cool walls of clay
the rooftree clay

carved from the hill's side
clumsy, uncompromising
all business and corners

scorched in the fire
the colors remember the flame
rust orange salmon inanimate rose

their fathers drove away the trees
only the crippled mesquite remains
good for nothing but the fire

their days are graceless
hard, identical
nights sudden and cold as knives

they huddle, dimly
the wick of reason lowered
a flickering fringe

it is their blood that glows
their laughter
harrowing the shadow

it is their flesh
that smoulders
blackening the ceiling

THE BARGAIN

The man carrying bricks
climbs past our window again
the bricks ride jostling in a sling on his back
flushed, arrogant
craning like tourists
they take the bloom off breakfast

he's set the band across his brow
incurious, he looks neither at us
nor where he's going
but at his desolate shoes

we know where he's going
the bricks have hired him
they come from down there
they want to see the sky
they all shook hands on the bargain
we do not enter

ascending, ascending
he thrusts his brow
against the load of ungrateful clay
we sit where we are
hands heavy with bread

BENEDICTION

Sunday morning the bells
he is drunk he is
bellowing drunk

it says in the book man is clay
he is more board than brick
more warped than broken

Saturday sundown he
crept from under his bricks
an empty vinegar bottle clenched in his fist

following his shoes to the corner store
for a loaf of bread
and a liter of light

he's set the bread aside
the bells the bells
this is his mass

his glasses are smeary and thick as
the bottle between his knees
he sweetens the bloodless grain with strawberry soda

he feels the dark knot tighten
sways to his feet and howls
not fluent ululu

but AI
AI
AI

pierced by the light
refuting the bells
and does a little goat dance out the gate

THE UNFINISHED ROOM

They lived in it as they laid it round them
course by course
roofed it over plastered painted swept

they fried their eggs on fires of broken scaffolding
laughing, cleaned the pan with bread
left us a crust

the naked wires reach like nerves from the receptacles
groping the gritty light
no spark leaps their desperate synapses

no glass in the frames
the wind comes in with the light
running her fingers over the sill

seeking a dry crust
asleep in its pan
like a forgotten god

THE STRANGER

On a bench in the plaza
under the barbarous trees
I chew my thumb and watch the girls go round
one way
the boys the other
a stranger in a town of strangers

in the market a man is selling his hands
they hang from his shirt like shameful meat
between us this uneasy peace
if he won't look in my pocket
I won't stare at his sleeves

the label in my shirt says
Do not maltreat me
I should paint it on my hat

and what are the children crying
the consonants spill from their tongues
like streams of colored pebbles
the names of their vowels are Warbler
Linnet Nightingale and Dove
here at last
I can say what I mean without fear
of being understood

HANDS

Hunched in your sunday suit
your grey face glides from the collar
uneasy ghost
you pass, wearing their hands
like pale armbands on the stiff black wool
mama's the right, old man's the other
you're truly ill

on the other side of the earth, a girl
runs to greet you
hair in flames
her hand reaches almost but never
touching yours
we paint such hands on our walls
to remind us

where are they taking you
holy family?

eyes wide
into your grief
shoes hardly kissing the pavement
you go without saying

BOY SINGING ON A BUS

Whose is he then?
the tired couple with the baby
will not admit to him
watching the dry scrub
stream past the window
like years of exile

he's singing into himself like a well
I hear only echoes
garbled, hollow

even his jacket disowns him
hunched behind him like a hump
the heavy shoulders are thinking of someone else
clutching the seat, his grey
ageless hand is all but lost
in the cavernous sleeve

still, someone's been at him lately
on his round shaved skull I surmise
the migrations of lice

and out of the wind
December sunlight brushing his lids
this is fine a place as any
in his bland, moony face
his eyes
are smiling shut

ALMS

for Amy

His knees drawn up to let me pass
he is small and miserable
as any man

his stick lies meek at his side
if he speaks it will rise and strike at the walk
pity will drool from the paving stones

he rattles a cupful of furious pencils
each one sharpened to its point
he holds out his fabulous sockets for me
to fill with silver

raptly my right good hand
like an enchanted eel
glides through my pocket
sweetness blooms in my heart and dies
a rose of blood
and for an instant I have more than I need

4

GENEALOGY

Fire was first
out of fire came fist
out of fist, teeth

teeth begat mouth
and mouth, stone
stone begat worm

worm took his tail in his mouth
and wind was born
out of wind came foot

foot begat running
running, water
water, womb

then
out of womb sprang meat
and meat went into his mother

and begat
and begat
and begat

GUIDE

I take you down
see the monster clam
pick up that stone

barefoot through washes of lye
tunnels of steamy tile
drowning in echoes
come with me

onto the rickety pier
fisherman's stilted shack
we half way there

last part nothing
through the trapdoor down
the ladder can't stop now falling
through rainbows of fish
you learn to breathe again

in no time
we here

look
I tease her
open for you

watch you fingers

IF HE COULD

I've tied my reason over my eyes
dog trails at my heels through the weeds

dog never asks *Why?*
only *Now?*
never *Where are we going?*
he drops his tail and follows his nose

if I could loosen with my miraculous forepaws
the furious knot at the back of my head
I'd tear the reason from my eyes
and send it flying

Now now dog would bark
look where you're going
this is the garden
there is the wall

Now he would howl
this is the beginning
here is the tree
give it a name
Earth-finger
Moon-beard, Sparrow-mother

here is the fruit
call it Good
the leaf, Green-tongue
Sky-feather
the sky, Star-meadow
where the dead worm flies
through the voice of the lark

if he could, dog would
And last he would say

If He Could

> *name me again*
> *Hail-fellow, Fast-companion*
>
> *Brother*
> *give you good morning*

FINDERS KEEPERS

In that tribe the priests are chosen
for memory alone
they have forgotten nothing
can give the gods their testimony
twelve nights running
chanting to each of the four winds in turn
that none be insulted

whereas the poets have memories
so frail
rising they remember neither
the nightmare nor the night before
wake without history
forebears
crying
ma ma
a lamb on a stone

each day
they construct anew
not merely their own
truncated lives
but the language of the tribe

KEEPING TIME

Can't keep time
not even time keeper
keeps it
trickles from his wrist
keeps running
hands keep
going round
game's not over
yet

listen
the Gahuku-Gama of New Guinea
play football some times
five days running
long as it takes
to reach a tie

time keeper there
keeps time on his drum
still it goes
BROOM it goes BROOM
it goes
BROOM
time keeper pounds time
he breaks it up on his drum
players play with the little pieces

FEEDING THE FIRE

The children know how to do it
they kneel to it tenderly
crooning, *Eat little fire
here is a scrap of paper, a handful of thorns*

and the moth knows
wrapped like a monk in saffron flame
and the log
serene in his iron cradle

now the fire has eaten the thorns
a girl approaches, gift outstretched
eyes averted, sidling warily
the fire snatches it from her hand

it has grown, it is
hungrier than ever

LILITH

She hissed in my ear
What can you lose?
she wasn't bad
but for the nose
that battle axe
long loose black hair
black arrogant eyes
generous mouth
great creamy boobs
on the frame of a boy
she laid for dwarves
and garbage men
fucked like a snake
beak like a hawk
held open house
in her round bed
without a foot
without a head

where is she now
slithering across what
littered moonscape
stirring with that
irreverent snoot
the dreams of virgins
dry gritty
snatches of spinsters
night lizard
demon of lonely sleepers
while we tumble and turn
in our four square bed
between us a field
a flock a house
two grumbling boys
twenty years
of sweat and bread
and everything to lose

CAIN'S SONG

First was Eve
the heavy mother
first the egg
cruising the borderless
kingdoms of water
gliding dividing
leaving herself behind
she was everywhere
coming and going
she met herself
she was bored
boredom is the root
of the sorry tree
I am the fruit

The air was not, nor the sky above it. What kept closing in?
Where? And whose enclosure? And was the plunging abyss all
water?

out of boredom
on her placid brow
heavy mother
grew a root
like a twisted horn
she looked about
there was no one
to bury it in
but herself
out of boredom she fell
into sleep
the root did not

And why shoulde I not commen more familiarly with you,
accordynge to my custome? I praie you, is it the head? the face?
the breast? the hands? or the eares? which parts of the body are
named honest, that engendre gods, and men? I trow no. Naie,
it is euien that selie membre, so fond, and foolisshe, as maie not

without laughter be spoken of, which is the onely planter of
mankynde. That, is the onely fountaine, whens all thynges receiue
life, a great deal sooner than from Pythagoras quaternion.

on her smooth brow
the twisted root
sprang to life
divided not quite
grew roots of his own
and leapt fully armed
with his hump and his flute
Adam the forked
Adam the clown

first was Eve
Adam the bone
he raised his flute
and played her awake
she swayed before him
watching the instrument
turn in his hand
to a tree to a snake
to a snail to a plow
he plowed a furrow
in the water
and called it land

Every so often this Humpback Flute Player would stop and
scatter seeds from the hump on his back. Then he would march
on, playing his flute and singing a song. His song is still remem-
bered, but the words are so ancient that nobody knows what they
mean.

thence to a lily
to an ear of corn
to a needle an arrow
an iron bar
he raised it high
about the tip

glinting swirled
a rose of dust
he brought it near
and stroked her breast
she felt her atoms
swivel in their flaming sockets
he called that direction

divided against
herself forever
heart against head
longing
loathing
heavy mother
took to her bed
he juggled it back
to a flute and played
her whole again
Adam the natural
Adam the clown

The syllables of a good double strophe are as follows: Zizozozizi-
zizizizizizirreuzipiah totototototototozissskutziah.

thence to a stick
beat time on her brow
thence to a feather
plunged in her belly
drew out a worm
she dreamed again
could feel us already
flailing away
with our knouts truncheons
nightsticks pikes
he called us Abel and Cain
things would never
be the same
heavy mother
moaned in sleep

Cain's Song

"It is a sound," say the Mullers, "that blends the deepest lowing of cattle with water splashing and something like sighs."

it is a sound
Cain will remember
till he dies

DEUS EX MACHINA

O Hermes 3000
hip grey messenger
god of thieves
what dark conspiratorial vowels
grim consonants
gather in your spools

I'm a god too
look
one stroke of my left hand
the paper rises, radiant
on a hill of keys

I run my fingers
over the white stones
seeking a way in

the paper
stiff, humorless
white as a parson's collar
rides back and forth
in his black carriage
taking notes

5

GETTING STARTED

Divest thyself you whisper
no way
the table digs his claws
into the rug
the chair won't leave
lamp's taken root

I wear the house like a stone shirt
kids scramble down my back
woman squats on my chest
like a red hot medal

Then empty thyself
how can I
I've eaten too many satisfaction cookies
birdsong drools from my ear
drunk to overflowing
I weep at the least provocation

how can I let in your voice
sweet silence
the cricket sits on my tongue
and fills my skull with his trivial music

MORNING SONG

In the crazed font, water
falls from my life with a sigh
I've seen her carrying trees in her beak
I've seen her drink the blood from a field

passed her in the harbor
dumb blue angel
pale wings draggled with grease
stood in the shadow and let her lick mud from my shoes

I knelt to kiss those foaming lips
I felt her tongue glide over mine
and down my throat
the dregs were familiar

what's not her in me is trash
she bears it away
each day, more and more
we become one another

AND SO IT FELL

We fell into our love like sleep
like water
sank through the clay
fear pulsing cool and thin as water
through blood red gills

the moon lay down in the mouth of our grave
like a stone
the thorns sprang up to hold us
we fell like petals
lip to lip
inside this mountain

ten years later who would find us
who would tear his flesh on thorns
to pluck us free

SAND

Wind flings it in my face
the mountain's broken teeth
ground to powder
washed beyond caring

does it remember the lamb
whose mild contemplative molars
nibbled the pastures bald
broke the back of the hill

goat was their shepherd
they did not want
dined on seedlings
and green shoots

while the land
slid
cautiously
out from under

ALL I EVER WANTED

All I ever wanted
haunts me
a trail in air
a memory in water

long since my hands
have learned its shape
reaching through sleep for it
arms outstretched
two beams
holding a coffin
over a grave

PROPHECY

All night the addict sits up in bed
writing letters
this one reads *Come in the water's fine*
this one *Help*

another *Mother water writhes in bed*
grinding her belly in the slime
wind licks the backs of her knees
I know what the stones play in the stream

one this morning *I've straddled the wave*
that runs before the destroyer like prophecy
that's my cord round your throat
cut me loose I'm sounding

the addict smiles takes up
his clear blue pencil titles it
PROPHECY
and files it away with the rest

THE HUNTER

Exhausted
all afternoon at the window
peering through the wrong end of his glasses

he can set his eye at the end of a straw
and sack the granary of the ant
he can flex each of his fingers separately

he has deafened the finch to see
if it still might sing
he has driven the wolf from its door

exhausted, tranquil
meat dreams in the market, asleep on its hook
the roses sleep with their backs to the wall

THE RACE

A boy I ran
in woods, where they couldn't see me
tripping over roots, through briars

my thighs ablaze with nettles
knees, twin wounds
weeping into my sneakers

when I broke into the open
leaping in great bounds
like jackrabbit, this-that-way

the trees stood at attention before me
in a double row
crossing their crooked wooden swords

at the end of the street in the ice-blue sky
the sun hangs low
the puddles take fire

my shoulderblades open and close behind me
lips of a bloodless wound
I shield my eyes, jog on

one ash-blonde leaf skips past me
into the schoolyard

the bell rang long ago

INTERVIEW WITH A WINNER

for Tom

What was it like?
like losing
same bloody feet
blazing tendons
same sweet release
melancholia of exhaustion

What did you win?
a chance

For what?
to do it again
that wasn't it
either

What did you get?
through

What's left for you?
tomorrow's race

losing is worse

COMING DOWN

All day up here sweating out
the lies that oil the works of love
if I had a million tongues I would lie to the grass

I give earth back nothing but her names
Mountain I mumble
old mouthful of stones
as if that might wake her from her trance

in my skull a red bird I can't name
folds his dark wings
the wind strays absently through the trees
riffling folios of light

all day up here
a local skirmish
strictly a holding action
between my fingers and the ledge

at sundown I descend to you dear heart
astonished to find you beating still

NEXT TIME

When I come back I want to be a rock.
                                                    Liza

Weary of uprightness
I would slouch like the cat
I would feign like the possum
hang by my tail like the leaf
lie in the dust like a stone
even as the least of these

surrounded by mirrors I am
always there before me
tired fighting over my shoulder
I would turn like the earth
that wretched stone
would look the cold
green moon in the eye
and sleep a millennium
nuzzled by the rain
licked by the sun

THE PETRIFIED LOVER

Reach me your hand
it has happened
atom by atom
slowly, it happens

feel where my pulse turns marble
my bones lime
garnets my blood
my heart obsidian, my eyes
brimming with milky opal
I would be tranquil as a stone

I would be grave as a stone
only the vines to hold me
climbing my shaft to the sun
rapt with hunger
thrusting their idiot fingers
in all my apertures

yet I go on singing
this brittle song
reaching my metamorphic arms
to take you in

FLUTE SONG

In the thin rain
the birds still flit
from limb to limb

the droplets gather
on the pane
deepening the blood
on the lips of the roses
etching the leaves
acid green

as I turn
the leaves begin
to tremble and dance

HAPPY BIRTHDAY

A carp, I dreamed a thousand years
in a cradle of water
what do I want with these knees?

an eon grunting in the shallows
drunk on ether
a season teaching my fingers to dance

somewhere behind me, time on time
history convulses
the ages of ice flash through my veins

I can smell it, that harsh medicinal light
why not?
next time I'll marry worms and father grass

I wonder what the dust hums
dancing in the sun
a mote in heaven's eye

FLYING SONG

Smoke on the wind
I travel light
my way is flight
my cries are music
a bowl of earth
a burning coal
and at my feet
the blessed weeds
the earth's sweet trash
are all I need

seed on the wind
I go alone
I light where I can
I stir the flowers
with my coal
and drink the smoke
the trash of trash
I'm nowhere long

a bowl for my hearth
the fire my friend
I fly when I can
and damn the cost
I think what I am
I know what I'll be
sweet trash sweet trash
in the roadside dust

THE WHEELCHAIR POET

for L.E.

1

Your house won't give you birth
sometimes it spills you out
to reel you in again
a mournful yo-yo

in the corner of your mouth
the spittle glistens
like unbidden poems

2

Your father wrought
to smooth your way
a front door ramp of weathered pine

I think of the shining pavement
the snail lays down
to ease his passage

3

Daddy built you in the cellar
a six day wonder
hammered you into these righteous angles
reinforced with tubular steel
ran this axle through your innominate bones
welded to your shoulderblades
these dandy aluminum handles

take them Mama
I want to feel
my tall wheels turning in their sockets

4

Perched on their shelf, your shoes
stiff, shining soles that never kissed a leaf

nor crushed an ant and licked his fiery blood
look up accusing as I take your hand

my street-wise brogans feel
the night-chill fluttering round their heels
little wings of wind

5
Pause at the door
here at the splintery lip of the ramp
November moonlight, thin as solvent
rinses the last oils from the roots of your hair

unhand me Mama
tonight I solo

6
She sets you on the inclined plane
to follow out
the hypotenuse of your helplessnesss
experiment whose end
was never in doubt

7
See how my light but serviceable frame
cants my spine to the precise
angle of my inclinations

with proper respect
for the ordinances of inertia
I gather speed

I open wide
my mouth my nostrils my eyes
to take it in

the bruised boards groan at their nails

8
He's nailed a board across my knees
for my Remington portable

I clutch in my hand the cool space lever
squeeze off bursts of hot lead syllables

by the time I hit the walk
it's all I can do
to skid round the end of the hedge
point my nose down the street
careening through late fall litter

the moon sails into my sights
a disembodied wheel
I clear all stops
and rise to intercept her

nightwind streams from the ends of my board
in silver tatters
my bright wheels kiss the flittering leaves
spinning off flakes of streetlight behind me
like tiny stars

Donald Finkel was born in New York City
and attended public schools there, notably
the Bronx High School of Science. He studied
sculpture at the Art Students League, and
after earning a B.S. in philosophy and an M.A.
in English at Columbia left the east for Illinois,
Iowa, and finally St. Louis, Mo., where he
is Poet in Residence at Washington University.
He has lived for several years in Mexico, and
travelled widely in the United States. He is
married and has three children, three cats,
and a beagle.

He is the author of *The Clothing's New
Emperor* (1959), *Simeon* (1964), *A Joyful
Noise* (1966), *Answer Back* (1968), *The
Garbage Wars* (1970), and *Adequate Earth*
(1972). He has been the recipient of a
Guggenheim Fellowship and a grant from the
National Endowment for the Arts. In 1974 he
received the Theodore Roethke Memorial
Award for the book-length poem, *Adequate
Earth*.